Island Songs

HAL•LEONARD UKULELE PLAY-ALONG

VOL. 22

CONTENTS

Lap Steel – Kenny Wilson   Piano – Lou Cucunato

Guitars – Mike DeRose   Whistle – Katy Marschke

Ukulele and all other instruments – Chris Kringel

Tracking, mixing and mastering by Chris Kringel

T0056517

ISBN 978-1-4584-2613-0

HAL•LEONARD® CORPORATION

7777 W. BLUEMOUND RD. P.O. BOX 13819 MILWAUKEE, WI 53213

Visit Hal Leonard Online at
www.halleonard.com

Bali Ha'i

from SOUTH PACIFIC
Lyrics by Oscar Hammerstein II
Music by Richard Rodgers

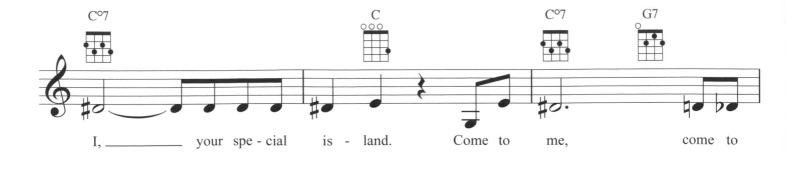

I, _____ your spe - cial is - land. Come to me, come to

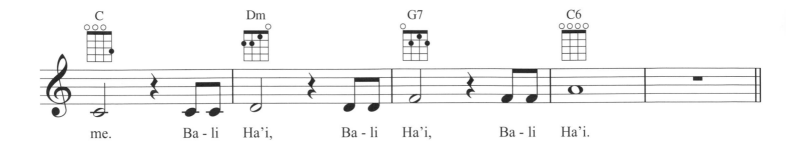

me. Ba - li Ha'i, Ba - li Ha'i, Ba - li Ha'i.

Bridge

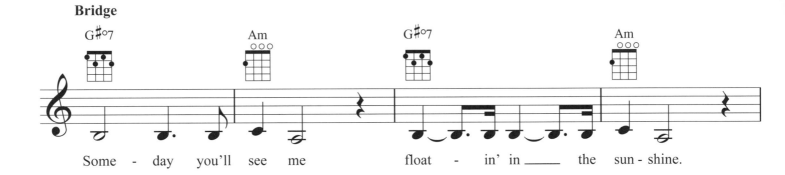

Some - day you'll see me float - in' in _____ the sun - shine.

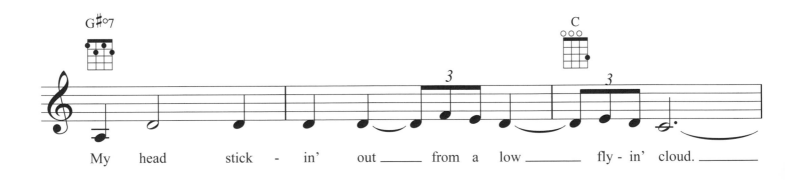

My head stick - in' out _____ from a low _____ fly - in' cloud. _____

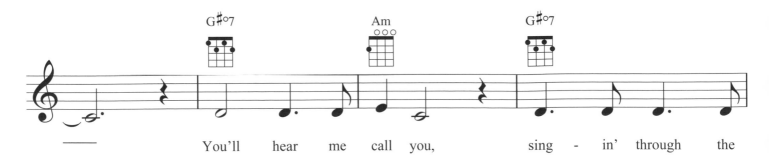

_____ You'll hear me call you, sing - in' through the

4

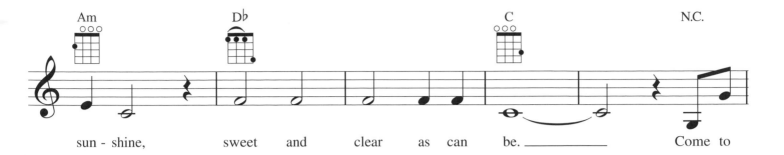

sun - shine, sweet and clear as can be. _____ Come to

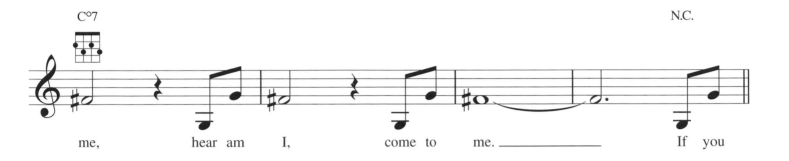

me, hear am I, come to me. _____ If you

Chorus

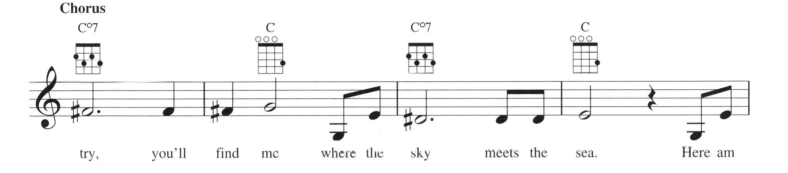

try, you'll find me where the sky meets the sea. Here am

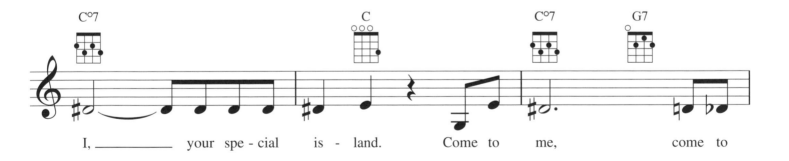

I, _____ your spe - cial is - land. Come to me, come to

Outro

me. Ba - li Ha'i, Ba - li Ha'i, Ba - li Ha'i. _____

The Breeze and I

Words by Al Stillman
Music by Ernesto Lecuona

TRACK 3

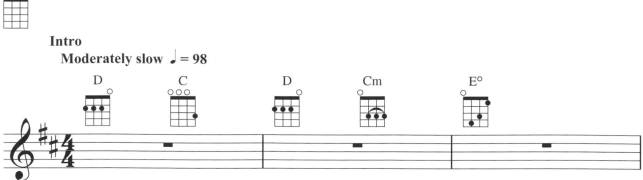

say - ing with a sigh _____ that you _____
whis - per - ing good - bye _____ to dreams _____

_____ no long - er care. _____ 2. The
_____ we used to share. _____

Bridge

Ours was a love song that

seemed con - stant as the moon, end - ing in a strange, mourn -

- ful tune; _____

Outro

and all a - bout me, they know you have de -

part - ed with - out me and we won - der

Play 3 times

1. why, _____ the breeze and I. _____
2., 3. I _____ the breeze and

Day-O
(The Banana Boat Song)

Words and Music by Irving Burgie and William Attaway

TRACK 5

First note

Intro
Moderate Calypso ♩ = 122

N.C.

Day - light come ___ and me wan' go home. ___

Verse

C

1. Work all night ___ on a drink of rum. ___

G7   C

Day - light come ___ and me wan' go home.

Stack ba - nan - a till de morn - ing come. ___

G7   C

Day - light come ___ and me wan' go home.

Day - light   come ____ and   me   wan'   go   home.
Day - light   come ____ and   me   wan'   go   home.

Six - hand,   sev - en   hand,   eight - hand   bunch.
Hide   the   dead - ly   black   ta - ran - t'la.

Day - light   come ____ and   me   wan'   go   home.
Day - light   come ____ and   me   wan'   go   home.

Chorus

Day,   me say day - o. ____   Day - light come __ and me

wan' go home.   Day,   me say day, me say day, me say...

Drifting and Dreaming

(Sweet Paradise)

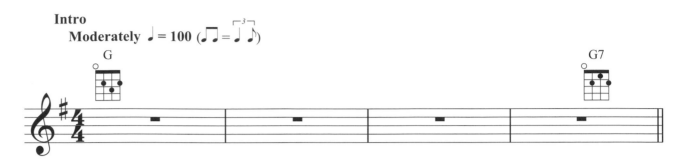

Words by Haven Gillespie
Music by Egbert Van Alstyne, Erwin R. Schmidt and Loyal Curtis

TRACK 7

First note

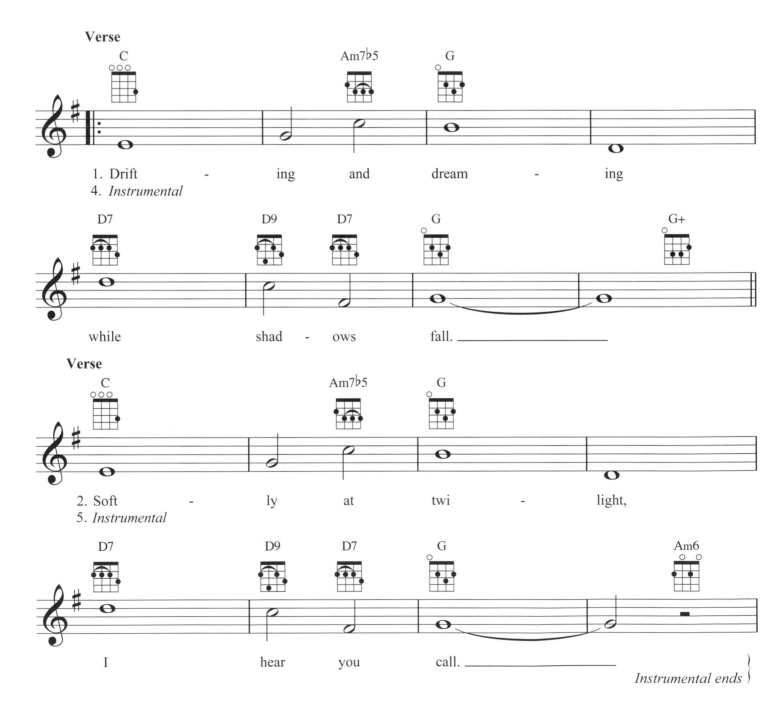

Bridge

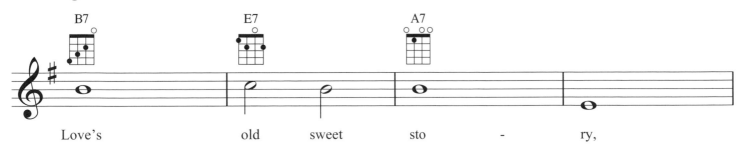

Love's   old   sweet   sto - ry,

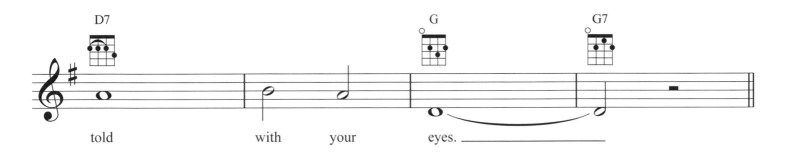

told   with   your   eyes.

Verse

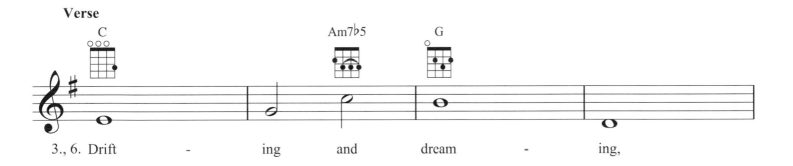

3., 6. Drift - ing   and   dream - ing,

1.

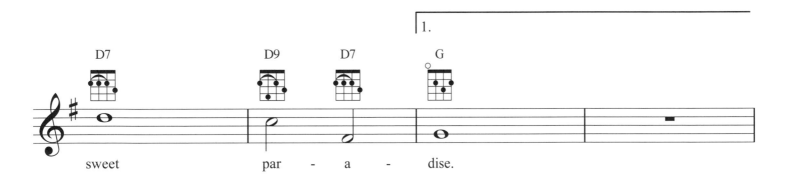

sweet   par - a - dise.

2.

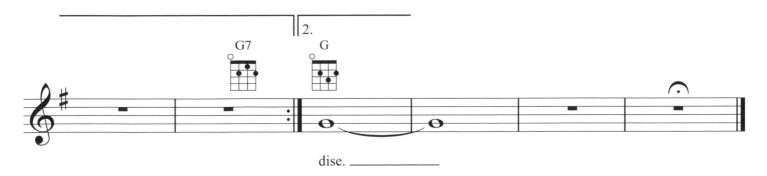

dise.

Jamaica Farewell

Words and Music by Irving Burgie

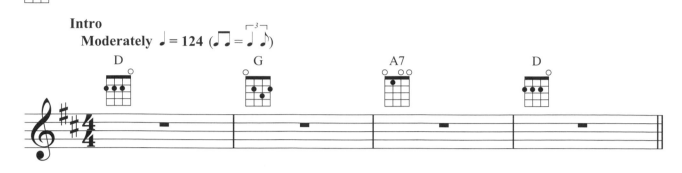

1. Down the way where the nights are gay ___ and the
2. Sounds of laugh - ter ev - 'ry - where ___ and the
3. Un - der the sea there can you hear ___ mer - folk

moon shines gai - ly on the moun - tain top,
danc - ing fish ___ sway - ing to and fro.
sing - ing songs ___ that I love so dear. ___

I took a trip on a sail - ing ship ___ and when I
I must de - clare my heart is there ___ though I've
Fish are danc - ing ev - 'ry - where ___ and the

reached Ja - mai - ca I made a stop.
been from Maine ___ to Mex - i - co. But, I'm
fun is fine ____ an - y time of year.

Chorus

sad to say, I'm on my way, ___ won't be back for

man - y a day. My heart is down, ___ my head is

turn - ing a - round, __ I had to leave a lit - tle crab in

King - ston town. __

Outro

TRACK 11

Limbo Rock

Words and Music by Billy Strange and Jon Sheldon

round   the   lim - bo   block.
like   a   lim - bo   tree.   Jack   be
fall   in   lim - bo   love.

lim - ber, Jack __ be quick,   Jack   go   un - der   lim - bo   stick.   All   a -

1.

To Coda

round   the   lim - bo   clock,   hey,   let's   do   the   lim - bo   rock.

Spoken: Limbo lower now,   limbo lower now.   How low can you go?   2. First,   you

2.

Chorus

do   the   lim - bo   rock.   La,   la,   la,   la,   la,   la, __ la,   la,   la,   la,   la,

la, la, la, ____ la, la. La, la, la, la, la, la, ____ la, la, la, la, la,

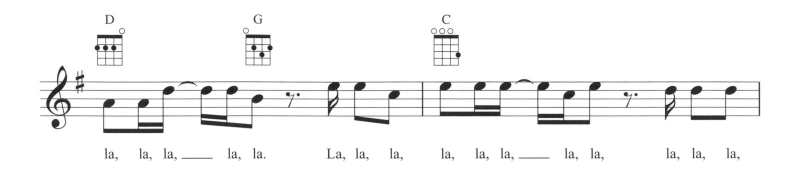

la, la, la, ____ la, la. La, la, la, la, la, la, ____ la, la, la, la, la,

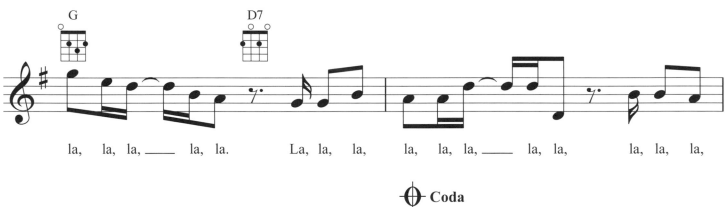

la, la, la, ____ la, la. La, la, la, la, la, la, ____ la, la, la, la, la,

Coda

D.S. al Coda

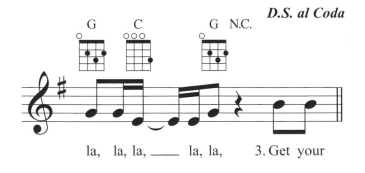

la, la, la, ____ la, la, 3. Get your

do the lim - bo rock.

Spoken: Don't move that limbo bar. *You'll be a limbo star.*

How low can you go?   La,   la,   la,

Outro-Chorus

la,   la,   la, ____ la,   la,   la,   la,   la,   la,   la,   la, ____ la,   la.   La,   la,   la,

la,   la,   la, ____ la,   la,   la,   la,   la,   la,   la,   la, ____ la,   la.   La,   la,   la,

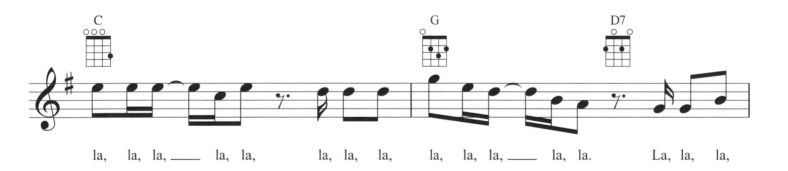

la,   la,   la, ____ la,   la,   la,   la,   la,   la,   la,   la, ____ la,   la.   La,   la,   la,

la,   la,   la, ____ la,   la,   la,   la,   la,   la,   la,   la, ____ la,   la.

The Moon of Manakoora

from the Motion Picture THE HURRICANE
Lyrics by Frank Loesser
Music by Alfred Newman

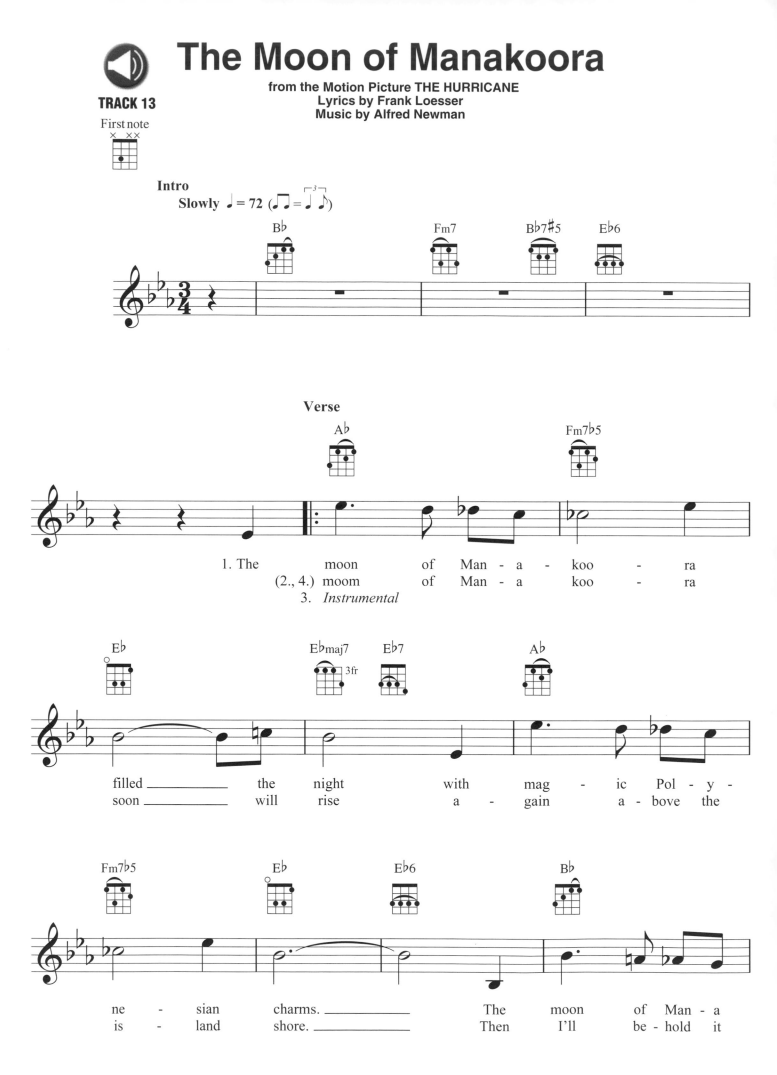

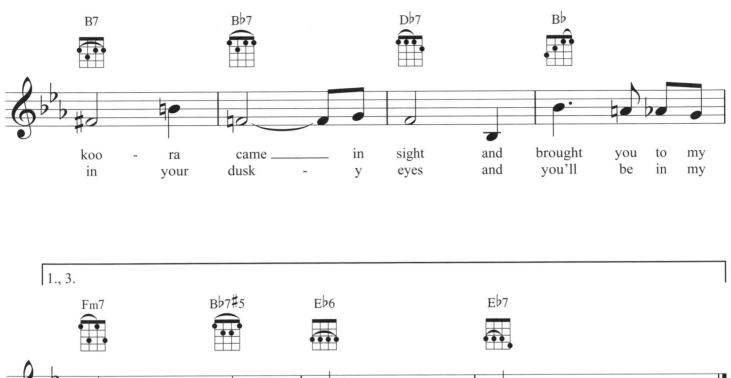

koo - ra came _____ in sight and brought you to my
in your dusk - y eyes and you'll be in my

1., 3.

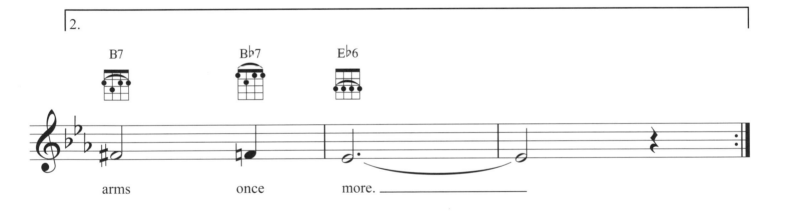

ea - ger arms. _____ 2., 4. The

2.

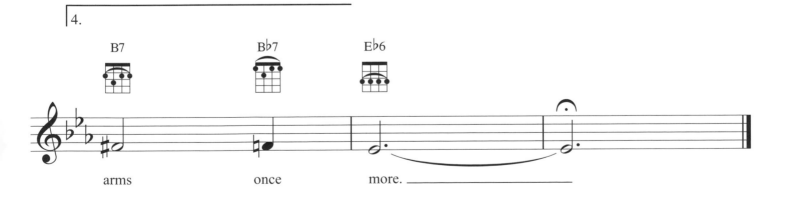

arms once more. _____

4.

arms once more. _____

Red Sails in the Sunset

Words by Jimmy Kennedy
Music by Hugh WIlliams (Will Grosz)

TRACK 15

Red sails in the sun - set,

I'm trust - ing in you.

Bridge

Swift wings you must bor - row;

make straight for the shore.

We mar - ry to - mor - row,

and he goes sail - ing no more.

Verse

3., 6. Red sails in the sun - set,

way out on the sea,

oh, car - ry my loved one

home safe - ly to me. me.